AURIC POLARIZATION
A HANDS ON GUIDE

JOHN VAN CRUMP

REIKI MASTER TEACHER
DOCTOR OF DIVINITY

2010

Order this book online at www.trafford.com
or email orders@trafford.com

Most Trafford titles are also available at major online book retailers.

First Printing

Cover Painting by C. VAN C.
Back cover photo by Evanna Cook
Illustrations by John Van Crump

Printed in the United States of America.

ISBN: 978-1-4269-5259-3 (sc)
ISBN: 978-1-4269-5260-9 (e)

Library of Congress Control Number: 2010918900

Trafford rev. 01/17/2011

 www.trafford.com

North America & international
toll-free: 1 888 232 4444 (USA & Canada)
phone: 250 383 6864 ♦ fax: 812 355 4082

DEDICATION

To God the one source with many names and to all my brothers and sisters around the world, a gift of Love and Light from my heart.

John Van Crump

ACKNOWLEDGMENTS

I thank my loving wife Charlene, my stepdaughter Evanna and my stepson's Orion and Mike for their assistance and support. I also thank my loving parents John and Christine Crump, and the rest of my family, Missy, Charlie, John Cook, Amber, Kristina, George, Lisa, Heide, Alicia, and my relatives and friends for their contributions to my life's path.

I thank Pamylle Greinke for introducing me to metaphysics and the book Your Healing Hands (The Polarity Experience) by Richard Gordon.

I thank Sarah Kavanagh for being a verifier of my experiences in the metaphysical world.

I thank Chris Milowski for sparking my interest in writing this guide, through his curiosity and desire to learn how to give an Auric Polarization.

I thank Antoinette Rehm for adding two important additions to this work by showing me how to fill my cup with Prana or Life-Force on page 90 position 38.

Table of Contents

Preface:

     I was lost in a world of confusion trying to understand what life was all about. I asked myself, "Who am I, and what is my purpose here?" After a serious car accident in 1986 I was paralyzed from the waist down. Rehabilitation restored my ability to walk but not the feeling in my legs. After a few more traumatizing incidents, and many failed relationships, I couldn't tell my feelings from any one else's. To dull these overwhelming feelings of helplessness I chose drugs like most people who experience emotional overload.

     After traveling many side streets in my life, I finally found the right road. I returned to college at the age of 40, and after graduation, I continued my education, but this time in metaphysics. In 1994 at a summer solstice party my legs were healed through someone who knew how to use energy, and the blocked nerve endings were re-stimulated. Once again I could feel the ground beneath my feet. It was at this time that I received my calling, to teach others through energy work so that they could heal themselves.

     I hope that this book will bring much Light and Love to all that use it. I am glad to be able to share with all my brothers and sisters on this Earth, the knowledge that is around all of us, and the joy of giving through your hands, the energy that is All.

John Van Crump

Introduction:

AURIC POLARIZATION

Auric Polarization or polarity energy balancing employs the currents that naturally flow through our hands. By connecting with another's current of life force, we can release blockages. Life force is the electro-magnetic energy field surrounding the body. When the energy of life force is flowing freely, we experience Joy, Love, Peace, Health, and Abundance. Alignment of the body's electro-magnetic energy field or aura takes place through physical and non-physical techniques and re-establishes the proper flow of life force throughout the entire body. Four different disciplines have been combined to achieve maximum results in realigning and releasing blockages in the four lower bodies. These disciplines are Reiki, Polarity, Shiatzu (accupressure), and Reflexology. These techniques relieve stress and bring deep relaxation to the body, while at the same time charging the cells in the body with life force, and strengthening the body.

Understanding Energy

Energy is the results of the movement of electrons and protons in every substance in the universe, known as electrical current flow between atoms.

To understand and feel energy, we must begin to recognize ourselves as an energy system. Everything in creation has its own vibrational frequency within its energy system. This is our own personal genetic code.

In the American culture the flow of energy is called Life-Force, in Chinese it is Chi, in Japanese it is Ki, in Polynesian it is Mana, in Greek it is Pneuma, in Hebrew it is Ruah, which means "Breathe of Life".

Bodies Energy Fields: The physical body is composed of many energy fields that surround it, emanate from it, and interact with the functions of the body. Some of the energies that emanate from the physical body are light (color), heat, sound, electricity, magnetism, and <u>electro-magnetism.</u>

Polarity: Polarity is a pattern in the universal law of nature. The law is that every substance in nature, the earth, and sun must have north and south magnetic poles. Everything that stands on the planet has a positive (+) charge at the top of their heads and a negative (-) charge at the base of their feet. The right hand has a positive (+) charge and the left hand has a negative (-) charge.

The Electro-magnetic Field: Scientific researchers call the electro-magnetic field the invisible bioplasmic body. The bioplasmic body is an invisible energy field that interpenetrates the visible physical body and extends beyond it about four to five inches. The word bioplasmic comes from bio meaning life and plasma, which is the third state of matter. Plasma is ionized gas,

gas that is charged with positive and negative particles (not the same as blood plasma). Bioplasmic body means a living energy body made up of invisible matter. Science, with the use of Kirlian photography is able to see and study this invisible body. The invisible system (the electro-magnetic field) is also known as the auric body. Within the auric body is the invisible etheric nervous system. Applying pressure to points on the body activates the energy flow from the invisible etheric nervous system to the body's physical nervous system. The Chinese word for the energy points on the body are called meridians and they are called nadis by the Hindus. Meridian and nadis points, when pressed, release trapped energy and permit that energy to flow freely through the pathways in the human body.

The Aura: The aura is an invisible energy field surrounding the body. There are three invisible energy fields in the bioplasmic body that make up the aura. The first field is the <u>inner aura</u> (etheric double); it follows the contour of the physical body. Its function is to absorb life-force energy into the body. The second field is the <u>health aura</u> which functions as a protective force field that shields the whole body from germs and diseased bioplasmic matter in the surroundings. The third is the <u>outer aura</u> and it extends about three feet from the physical body. It is a force field, which contains the aura and prevents life-force from leaking out of it. These three energy fields make up the whole aura, which is usually multi-colored and shaped like an inverted egg.

The Chakras: The chakras are whirling energy centers that control and supply energy to the vital organs of the physical body. When energy is blocked in the electro-magnetic field or aura, it causes stress to build in one or more of the seven energy centers or chakras. The colors of the chakras are influenced by the etheric (spiritual), emotional, mental, and physical states of the person.

1. **Base or Root Chakra:** This chakra is located at the base of the spine or at the coccyx area. Its color is <u>red</u>, the element is <u>earth</u>, and the energy state is <u>solid</u>. It energizes and strengthens the whole body and is responsible for our physical well being. It deals with survival, grounding, and the emotional state of calmness. When this chakra is blocked, our glands do not receive enough vital energy. This can cause problems in the legs, bones and large intestines, resulting in hemorrhoids, constipation, degenerative arthritis, anorexia, obesity, sciatica, and frequent illness.

2. **Sacral or Sexual Chakra:** It is located below the navel and above pubic area. Its color is <u>orange</u>, the element is <u>water</u>, and the energy state is <u>liquid</u>. It controls and energizes the sexual organs and the bladder. Chakra two deals with desire, pleasure, sexuality (your lower creativity), and the emotional state of tears. When blocked, it effects these glands, ovaries, prostate and the testes, causes problems in the womb, genitals, kidneys, bladder and circulatory system. Lack of energy to these organs, results in impotence, frigidity, kidney, uterine, and bladder trouble.

3. **Solar Plexus Chakra:** It is located above the navel and below the sternum. The color of this chakra is <u>yellow</u>, the element is <u>fire</u>, and its energy state is <u>plasma</u>. This chakra energizes and controls the pancreas, liver, stomach, large intestine, the appendix, the diaphragm and to a certain degree, the small intestines. The heart is greatly affected by this chakra. The solar plexus chakra is an energy clearinghouse center for the lower and higher chakras. <u>Energizing this chakra can strengthen the whole body.</u> This chakra deals with the will power, and the emotional states of laughter, anger and joy. Blocked energy can cause malfunctions in the pancreas and the digestive system, resulting in ulcers, diabetes and hypoglycemia.

4. **Heart Chakra:** It is located at the center of the chest. The color is green, the element is air, and the energy state is gas. It controls and energizes the heart, lungs, the thymus gland and the circulatory system. This chakra deals with love, balancing and the emotional state of compassion. When energy is blocked it affects the physical heart, lungs, the thymus gland and blood circulation. This causes problems like asthma, high blood pressure, stroke, and heart dis-ease.

5. **Throat Chakra:** It is located at the throat. The color is blue, the element is sound, the energy state is vibration. The throat chakra controls and energizes the hypothalamus, throat, thyroid, and parathyroid glands. This chakra deals with communication, creativity and the emotional state of connection. When the chakra is blocked it effects the ears, throat, mouth, neck, shoulders, arms, and hands. Blocked energy flow causes sore throats, stiff necks, colds, hearing, thyroid, and speech problems.

6. **Ajna or Third Eye Chakra:** It is located at the area between the eyebrows. The color is indigo, the element is image, the energy state is light. It energizes and controls the pituitary gland, and it also energizes to a certain degree, the brain. It is also called the master chakra, because it directs and controls the other chakras, plus the corresponding endocrine system. This chakra deals with intuition, imagination and its emotional state is dreaming. Blockage in the pituitary gland affects the eyes, and can cause blindness, headaches, nightmares, eyestrain and blurred vision.

7. **Crown Chakra:** It is located at the top of the head. Its color is violet, the element is thought, the energy state is information. It controls and energizes the brain and the pineal gland. This chakra deals with understanding, knowing and the emotional state of bliss. The pineal gland when blocked affects the central nervous system, the cerebral cortex and can cause depression, alienation and confusion.

We deal and comprehend life through four systems; called the four lower bodies:

1. **The Emotional Body** is the feeling world. It is the largest of the four systems, and it is composed, primarily, of the water element.

2. **The Mental Body** is the vehical of consciousness, the instrument of the soul and the "Thinker" of the average human being. It manifests itself through the emotional and physical systems.

3. **The Etheric Body** is an energy system composed of force centers and "nadis." Its function is to store up life-force, radiating light and heat from the Sun and to transmit them, via the spleen, to all parts of the physical body.
    These functions are primarily:
    1. To receive Life-Force into the body
    2. To assimilate it
    3. To transmit it

4. **The Physical Body** is the anchorage for the seven chakras upon the Earth through which the energy of Life Force should be channeled. When these systems are in perfect attunement, we have perfect health, peace, joy, and abundance in our life.

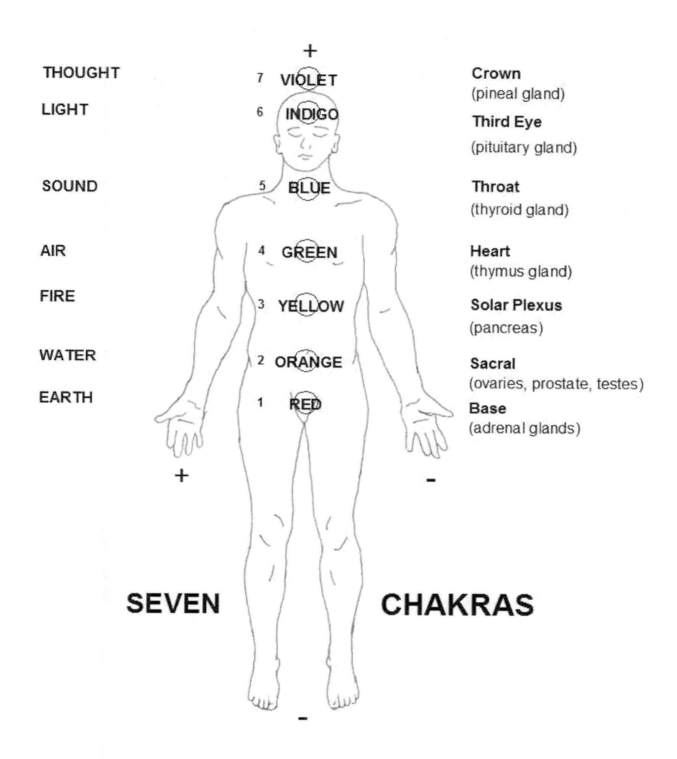

THOUGHT + 7 VIOLET Crown
(pineal gland)

LIGHT 6 INDIGO Third Eye
(pituitary gland)

SOUND 5 BLUE Throat
(thyroid gland)

AIR 4 GREEN Heart
(thymus gland)

FIRE 3 YELLOW Solar Plexus
(pancreas)

WATER 2 ORANGE Sacral
(ovaries, prostate, testes)

EARTH 1 RED Base
(adrenal glands)

+ -

-

SEVEN   CHAKRAS

MAJOR ORGANS OF THE **HUMAN BODY**

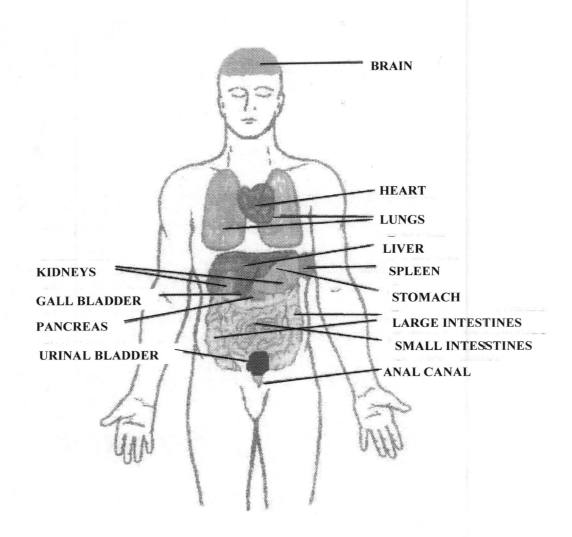

BRAIN

HEART

LUNGS

LIVER

SPLEEN

STOMACH

KIDNEYS

GALL BLADDER

PANCREAS

URINAL BLADDER

LARGE INTESTINES

SMALL INTESSTINES

ANAL CANAL

How to feel energy:

Rub your hands together for about ten seconds and place your palms two inches apart. Slowly move your hands apart six inches and then move back to the two inch point. You will feel a tingling or heat emanating from the palms of your hands. This is what excited ions or energy feels like. This emanating energy is used in Auric Polarization and other energy work, such as getting rid of headaches and relieving emotional overload.

Before we can apply this energy, we must understand the energy we feel is an electrical current of negative and positive polarities flowing from one hand to the other. Energy is not bad or good. It is the law of nature that opposites attract each other. Just as the earth has opposite poles north (positive) and south (negative), humans do also. At the head is the positive pole; at the feet is the negative pole. The right hand is positive and the left hand is negative.

Getting rid of a headache:

Stand to the left of the person. Have the person lay or sit still, close their eyes, and breathe deeply.

Rub your hands together for about ten seconds. Place your left palm (-) two inches away from the person's forehead at **point 1.** Place your right palm (+) on the middle of the base of the person's neck at **point 2**. Hold your hands in this position approximately twenty (20) seconds. You may feel heat, cold, vibration, or pulsation, depending on the person and you, as you first place your hands on them. The energy will lessen in intensity as the blocked energy, causing the headache, is released. The proper flow of electro-magnetic energy is then restored to normal.

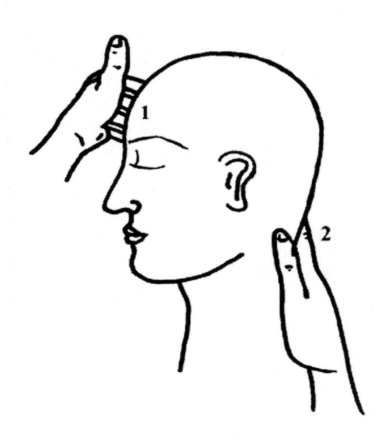

Trauma drain for releasing emotional overload:

Stand behind the person, rub your hands together, place your left palm down on the end of the person's left shoulder, place your right palm down on the end of the person's right shoulder. Tell the person to stand still, close their eyes, and breathe deeply. Hold this position until the person calms down. You'll know the person is calm when their shoulders sink down.

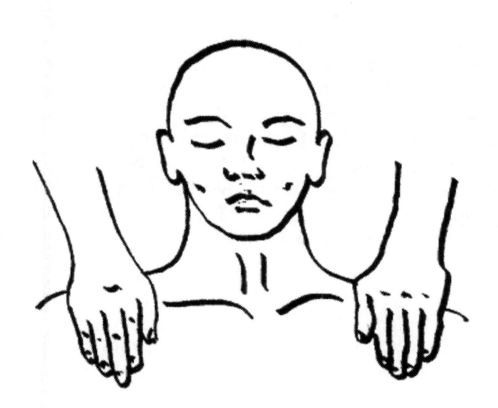

Simple Auric Wipe Down and Sealing of the Aura

An Auric Wipe Down is a downward movement of your hands from the top of the person's head to their feet with your hands approximately four (4) inches from the person's body. Shake your hands vigorously afterwards, to remove the person's bio-plasmic debris from your hands.

Have the person stand facing you; place your hands side by side with your thumbs touching each other palms down, about four inches above the person's head at **POINT 1**. Wipe down meridian **1** to the feet three (3) times. Repeat this move at the back of the person. These moves cleanses the aura

Sealing the Aura involves two movements, **#2** for the inner body and **#3** for the outer body. Return to the front of the person. Spread your hands approximately six (6) inches apart, palms facing each other at **POINTS 2** at the sides of the person's feet. Wipe up the inner body of the person to **POINTS 2** at the sides of their head to seal the inner body. Then wipe down the outer body **POINTS 3** from the person's head to their feet. This final movement completely seals the person's whole aura. Shake your hands when you are finished.

SIMPLE WIPE DOWN AND
SEALING THE AURA

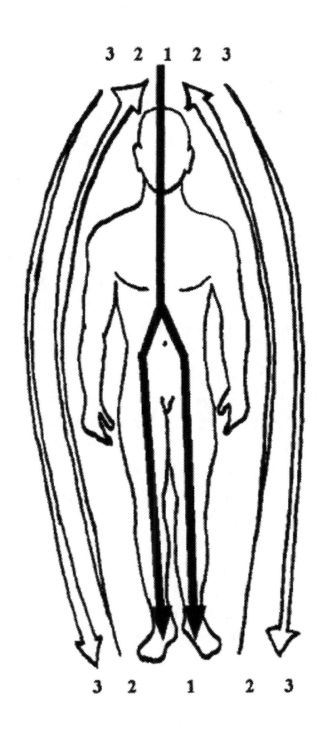

IMPORTANT

Before doing an AURIC POLARIZATION it is most important to set yourself aside. We are <u>channels</u> for healing to take place. We are not the ones doing the healing. It is the individual that heals himself or herself.

When you are ready to begin an AURIC POLARIZATION, call upon your Higher Power to assist you. You can simply say, "I am calling forth the healing Love and Light from the Source of all Being to assist me now to do what has to be done in this situation."

By setting yourself aside, you remove yourself from the other person's karma. Taking in someone else's burden can leave you drained and open to dis-ease. This is why it is also important to <u>wash your hands in cold water</u> before and after **EVERY** session; otherwise the bio-plasmic debri will build up in your aura like static electricity, muddying up your aura and your ability to be an effective channel for healing.

It is also a good practice to smudge the room you are working in both before and after a session. You can buy whole sage at most Health Food Stores. Smudging is a Native American practice used for purification of atmosphere and persons. Light the sage; put out the flame and swing the smoking sage around in a counter-clockwise motion in all four directions or corners of the room and doorways. This sets up much needed negative ions that help uplift us bringing feelings of well-being.

Follow these three rules for AURIC POLARIZATION THERAPY and you can never go wrong.

    1. Setting yourself aside.
    2. Washing your hands in cold water.
    3. Smudging.

AURIC
POLARIZATION

POSITION 1

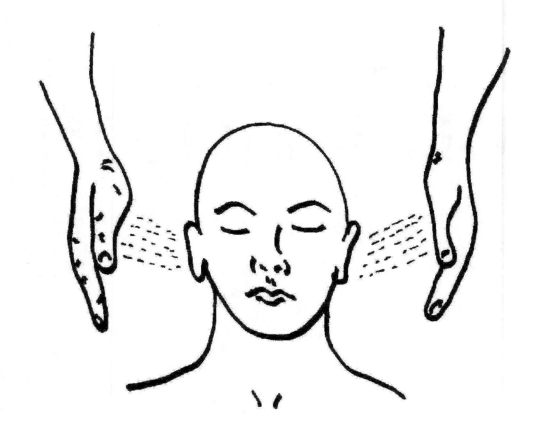

POSITION 1: Place hands on each side of person's head. Concentrate on Chi energy coming out of the palms of your hands and into the person's head. Hold this position for one minute. (This aligns the crown chakra at the top of the head, and balances the right and left hemispheres of the brain).

POSITION 2

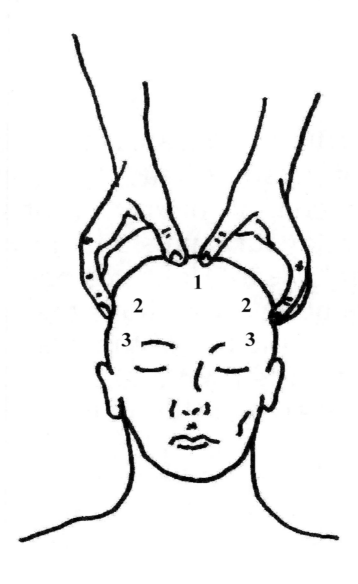

POSITION 2: Press **POINT 1** on the crown of the head with thumbs three (3X) times. Place thumbs on **POINT 1** at crown of head, and place fingertips at the sides of the head at **POINTS 2.** Hold this position for three (3) seconds. Press **POINT 1** on the crown with thumb three (3x) more times. Then place thumbs on **POINT 1** at crown and fingertips at the sides of the head at **POINTS 3**, above the ears. Hold this position for three (3) more seconds.

POSITION 3

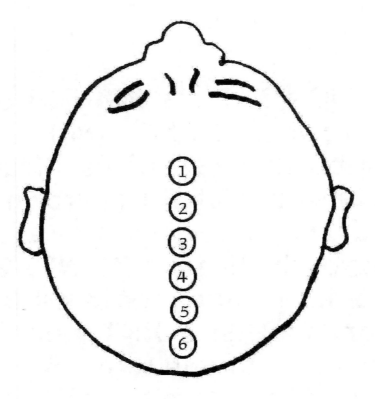

POSITION 3: Press shiatzu
POINTS 1 through **6** on top of
head with both thumbs
simultaneously. Hold each point
three seconds.

POSITION 4

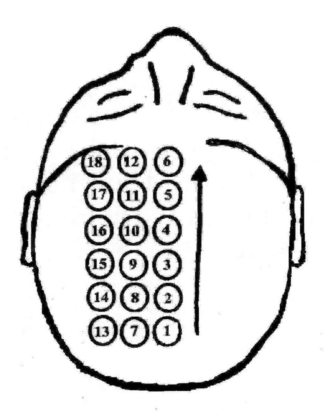

POSITION 4: Hold right side of head with right hand while pressing **POINTS 1** through **18** on the top of left side of the head with your left thumb. Hold each point three (3) seconds. Now hold the left side of head with your left hand while pressing **POINTS 1** through **18** on top right side of head with right thumb. Hold each point three (3) seconds.

POSITION 5

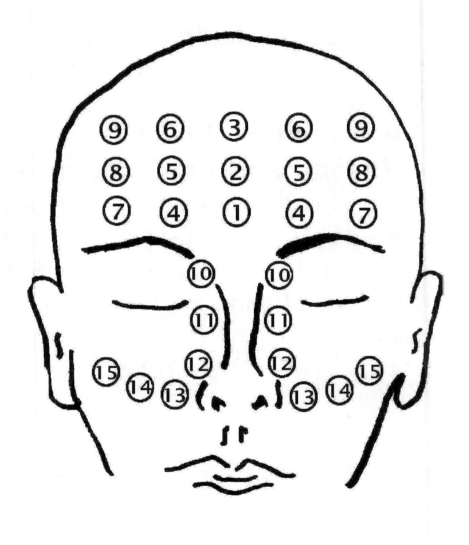

POSITION 5: With pointer fingers together, simultaneously press **POINTS 1, 2 & 3** on the forehead. Hold each point three (3) seconds. Spread pointer fingers apart and simultaneously press **POINTS 4** through **9** on both sides of forehead. Hold each point three (3) seconds. Press lightly with pointer fingers **POINTS 10, 11 & 12** along both sides of the nose. Hold each point three (3) seconds. Press **POINTS 13, 14 & 15** on both cheeks with pointer fingers. Hold each point three (3) seconds.

POSITION 6

POSITION 6: Simultaneously place middle fingers at the corners each eye and lightly hold each point three (3) seconds. Press both jawbone joints under the ears at **POINTS 1** with middle fingers. Hold (3) three seconds. Continue pressing with fingertips **POINTS 2** through **6** along the bottoms of both sides of the jaw, holding each point for three (3) seconds. Reverse and go from **POINT 6** back down to **1**. Hold each point three (3) seconds.

POSITION 7

POSITION 7: Hold earlobes between thumbs and pointer fingers at **POINTS 8** and gently pull down on lobes. Hold for one (1) second. Place thumbs at the tops of each ear between **POINTS 2 & 3** gently pushing the ears down. Hold for one (1) second. Place thumbs on the inside of each ear at **POINTS 5** and gently push the ears down. Hold one (1) second.

Place fingertips at the back of each ear at **POINTS 5** and gently pull the ear up. Hold for one (1) second.

POSITION 8

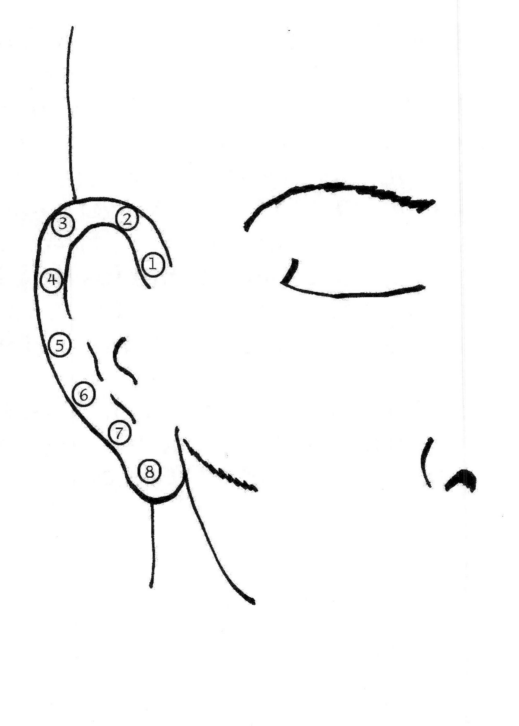

POSITION 8:   Simultaneously press **POINTS 1** through **8** around each ear between thumbs and middle fingers. Hold each point one (1) second. Hold each earlobe at **POINT 8** between thumbs and middle fingers and gently pull the earlobes down three (3x) times.

POSITION 9

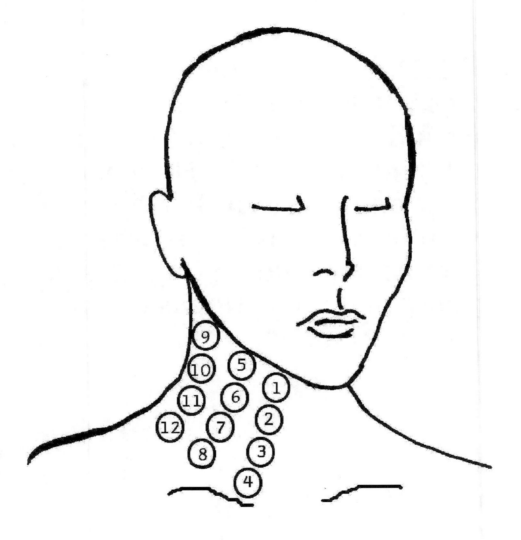

POSITION 9: Simultaneously press **POINTS 1** through **12** on front and sides of neck with middle and ring fingers of each hand. Hold each point three (3) seconds.

POSITION 10

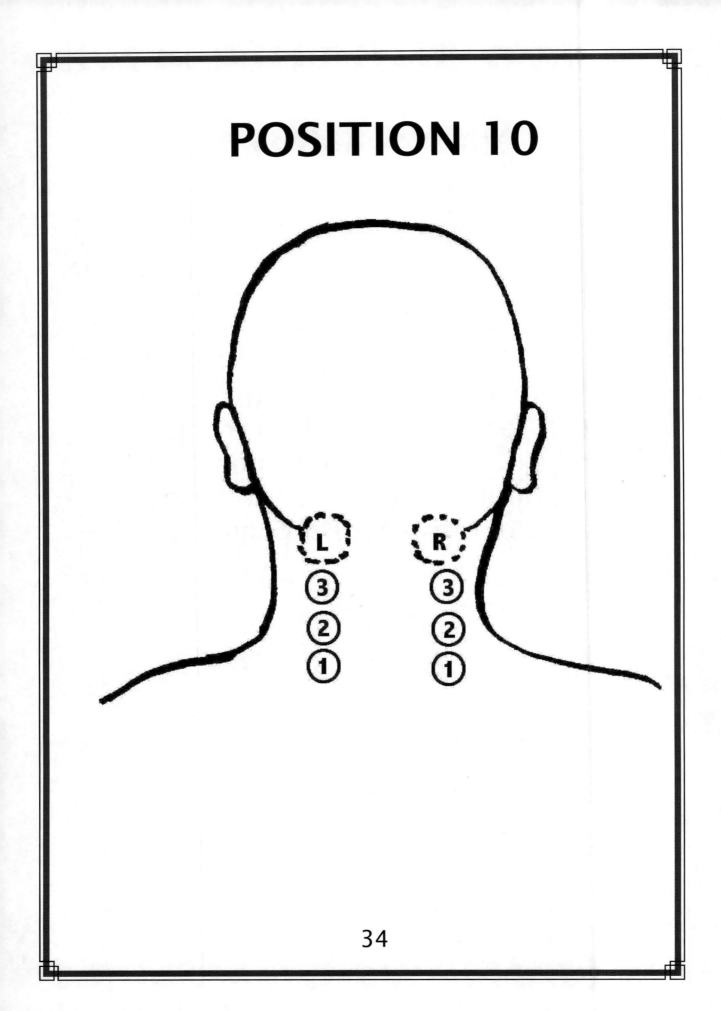

POSITION 10: Simultaneously press and massage **POINTS 1, 2 & 3** on back of neck with middle and ring fingers of each hand. Hold each point three (3) seconds. Cup hands around back of neck and place fingertips into the occipital cavities (**L & R**), pulling towards yourself. (Tell the person to breathe deeply). Hold this position for four (4) seconds.

POSITION 11

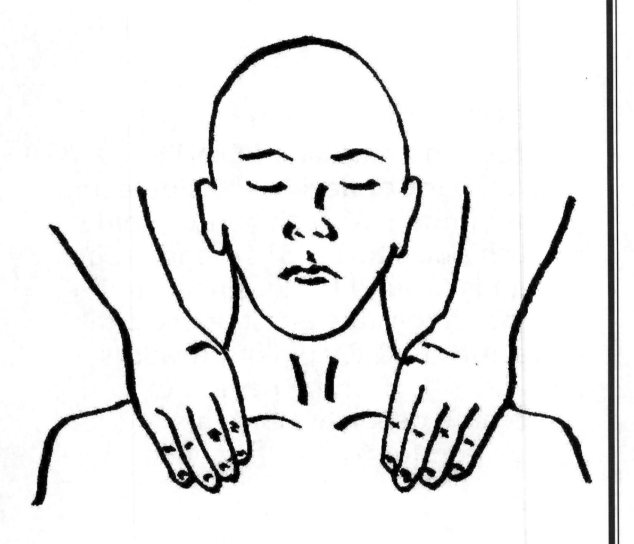

POSITION 11: Rub your hands together and place thumbs on the seventh (7th) vertebrae (base of the neck) and place fingers over the person's collar bones. Hold three (3) seconds.

POSITION 12

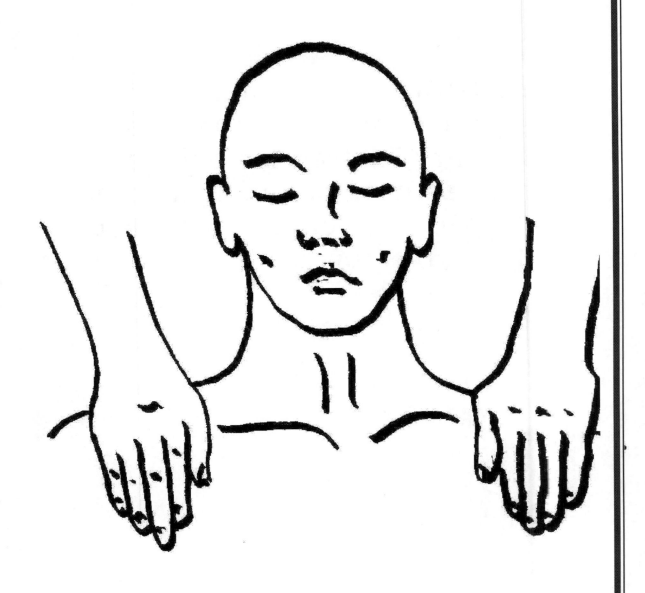

POSITION 12: Rub your hands together and place palms on the ends of the person's shoulders. Hold this position for seven (7) seconds.

POSITION 13

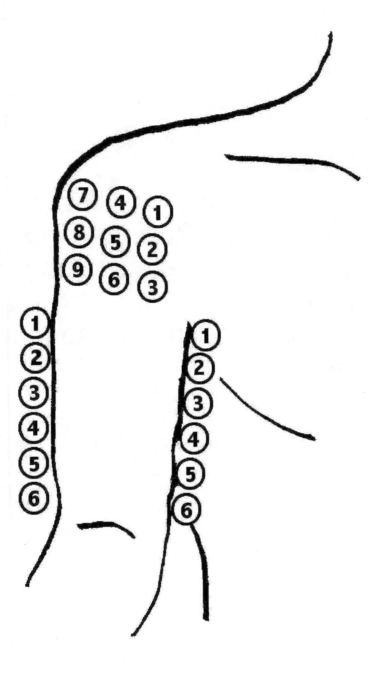

POSITION 13: Press **POINTS 1** through **9** on the right shoulder with right thumb. Hold each point three (3) seconds. Place right middle finger on outside of arm and thumb on inside of arm under armpit. Press **POINTS 1** through **6** inside and outside upper arm simultaneosly. Hold each point three (3) seconds.

POSITION 14

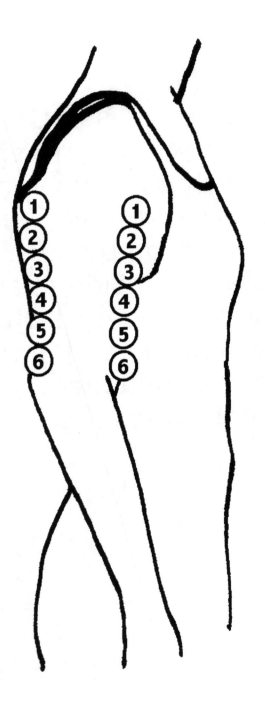

POSITION 14: Place left middle finger at back of arm and thumb at front of arm. Press **POINTS 1** through **6** on front and rear of upper right arm simultaneously. Hold each point three (3) seconds.

POSITION 15

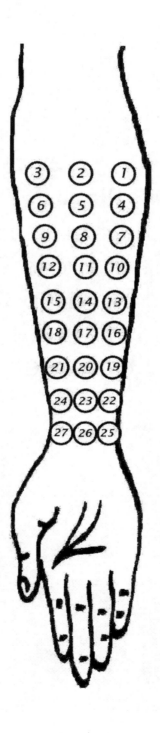

POSITION 15: Press **POINTS 1** through **27** inside right forearm with right thumb. Hold each point three (3) seconds.

POSITION 16

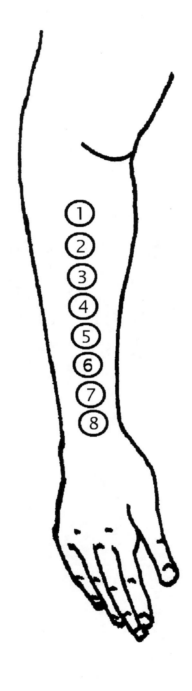

POSITION 16: Press **POINTS 1** through **8** on top of the right forearm with left thumb. Hold each point three (3) seconds.

POSITION 17

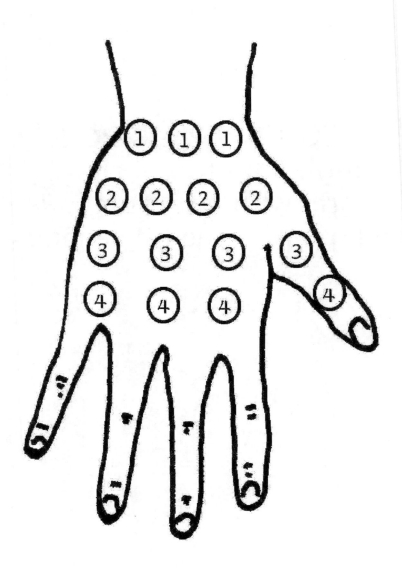

POSITION 17: Press **POINTS 1** through **15** on back of hand with right thumb. With both hands massage right shoulder, upper arm, forearm and hand. Hold right wrist in left hand and with right hand wipe down the person's right thumb and fingers.

POSITION 18

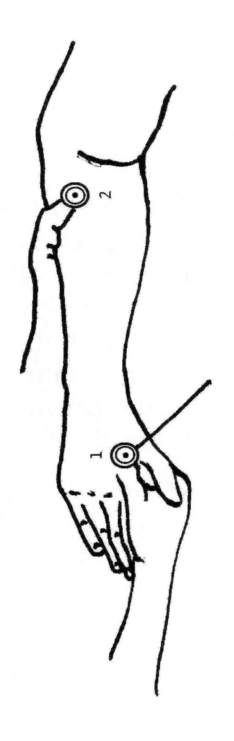

POSITION 18: Simultaneously press **POINTS 1 & 2** on the right arm with thumbs. Press points three (3x) times.

POSITION 19

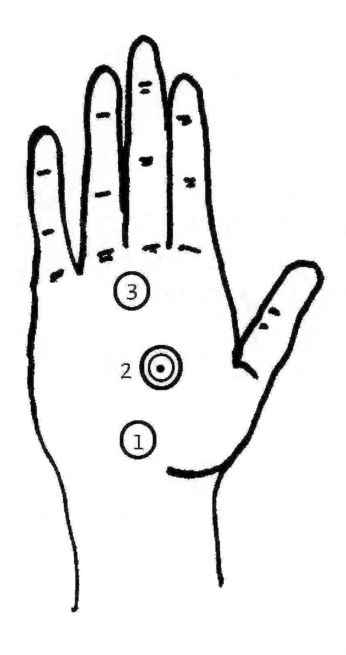

POSITION 19: Place person's right hand palm up. Press and hold **POINTS 1, 2 & 3**. Hold each point one (1) second. Hold right forearm in left hand, then vigorously shake person's right thumb and fingers.

Place hands together at right side of head and wipe down neck, shoulder, arm, hand, and finger tips. (Shake hands well to release static electricity build up).

Repeat on the left shoulder, arm, and hand.

POSITION 20

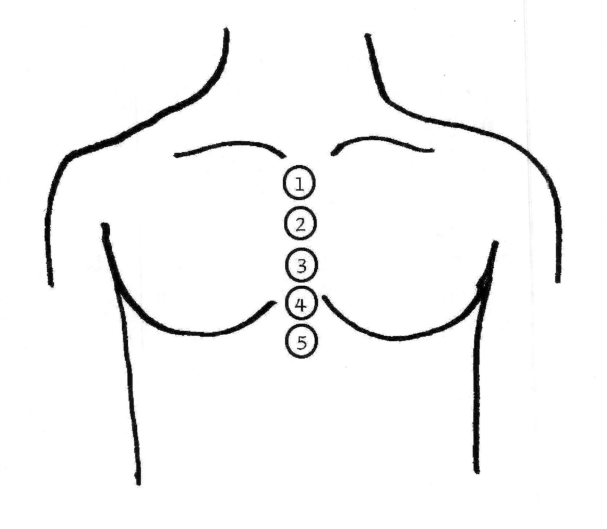

POSITION 20: Return to person's right side and press **POINTS 1** through **5** on the sternum with right thumb. Hold each point for three (3) seconds.

POSITION 21

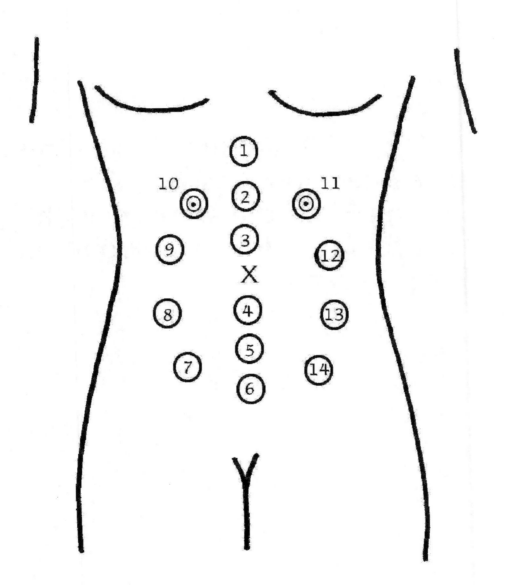

POSITION 21: Press **POINTS 1** through **14** around the stomach with right thumb. Hold each point three (3) seconds.

POSITION 22

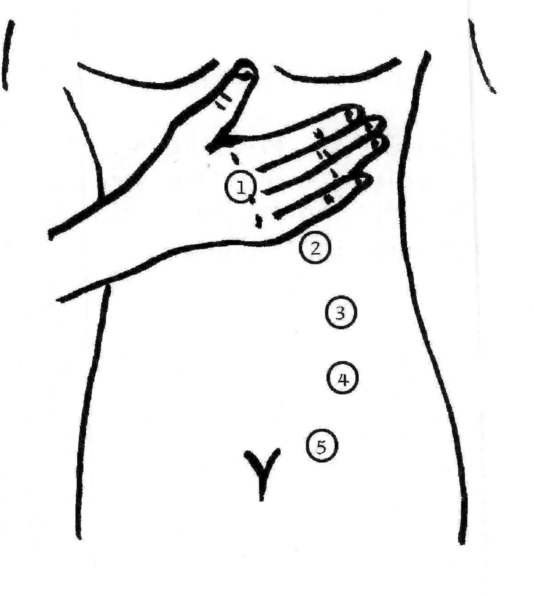

POSITION 22: Rub your hands together and place right palm on **POINT 1** at solar plexus. Hold point for thirty (30) seconds. (Shake your hands). Place right palm on **POINTS 2** through **5**. Hold each point three (3) seconds. (Shake your hands after **POINT 5**).

POSITION 23

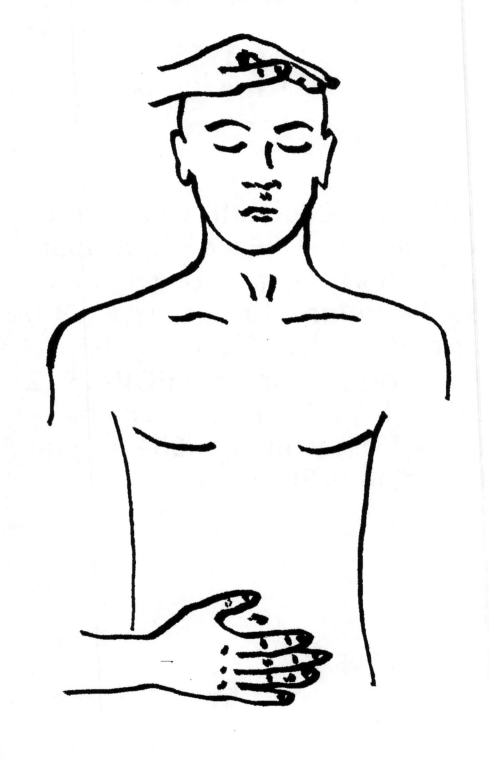

POSITION 23: Rub your hands together and place left palm on crown of person's head. Place right hand 3 inches below naval and rock person's hips back and forth (4) times. Stop and hold for seven (7) seconds. Raise your hands (3) inches above person's naval and head. Hold this position for three (3) seconds.

POSITION 24

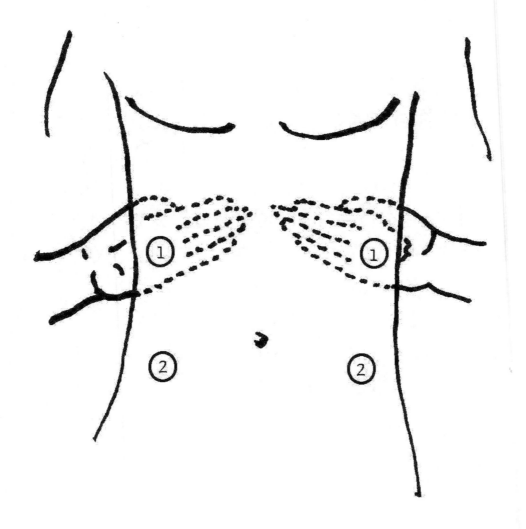

POSITION 24: Rub your hands together and place palms under person's back at **POINTS 1**. Hold these points three (3) seconds. (Shake your hands). Rub hands together again, place palms under person's back at **POINTS 2**. Hold these points three (3) seconds. (Shake your hands again).

POSITION 25

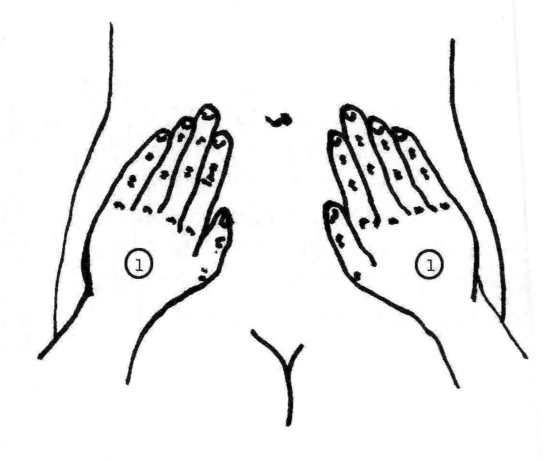

POSITION 25: Rub your hands together and place palms on **POINTS 1**. Place right palm on person's left hip, the left palm on their right hip. Hold this position (3) seconds. (Shake your hands).

POSITION 26

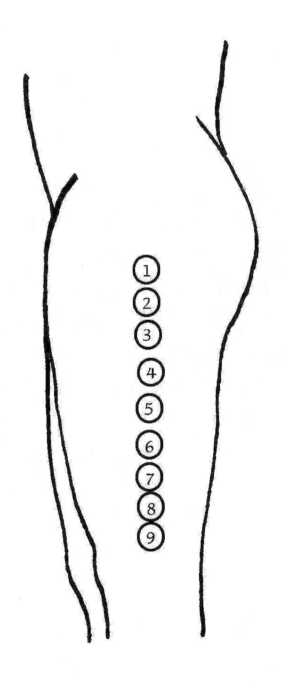

POSITION 26:   Simultaneously press **POINTS 1** through **9** on outside of each thigh with middle and ring fingers. Hold each point three (3) seconds.

POSITION 27

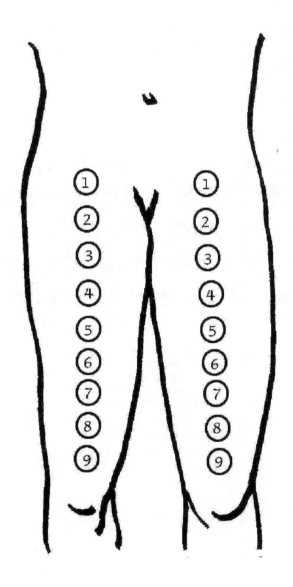

POSITION 27: Simultaneously press **POINTS 1** through **9** on top of each thigh with thumbs. Hold each point three (3) seconds.

POSITION 28

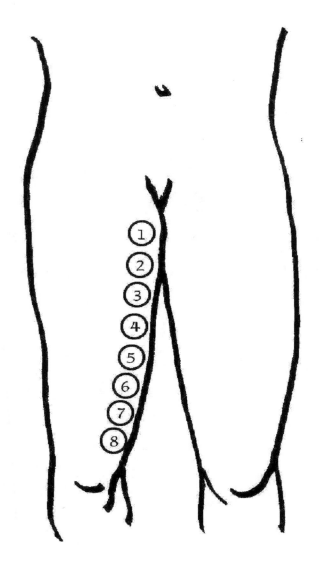

POSITION 28:   Place left palm on outside of person's right thigh and press **POINTS 1** through **8** on the inside of the right thigh with right thumb. Hold each point for three (3) seconds. Repeat on inside of the left thigh, pressing **POINTS 1** through **8** with left thumb. Hold each point for three (3) seconds.

POSITION 29

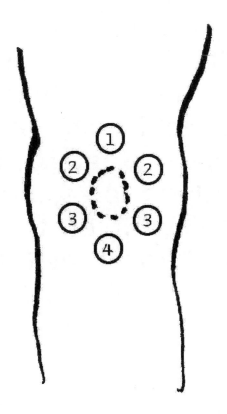

POSITION 29: Simultaneously press **POINTS 1** at the top of the kneecaps. Press left thumb on right knee and press right thumb on left knee. Hold both points for three (3) seconds. Press **POINTS 2** with thumbs and middle fingers. Hold for three (3) seconds. Press **POINTS 3** with thumbs and middle fingers. Hold for three (3) seconds. Press **POINTS 4** with thumbs holding three (3) more seconds. Rub hands together and place them over both knees and rock the knees back and forth four (4x) times.

POSITION 30

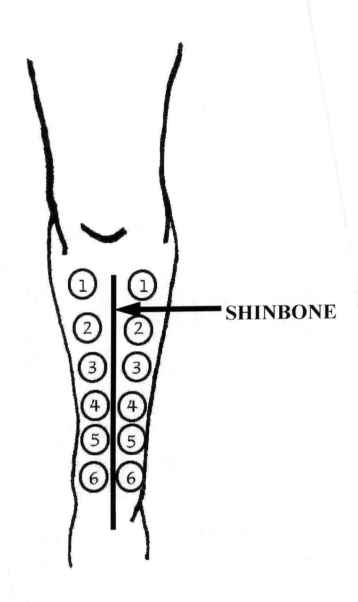

SHINBONE

POSITION 30: Simultaneously press **POINTS 1** through **6** on both calves, with thumbs on the inside, and middle fingers on the outside. Hold each point three (3) seconds.

POSITION 31

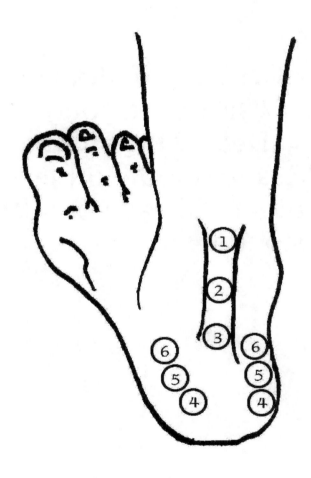

POSITION 31: With left hand, lift right foot by the toes and press **POINTS 1, 2 & 3** on the Achilles tendon with right thumb on the outside and right pointer finger on the inside. Hold each point three (3) seconds. Press **POINTS 4, 5,** and **6** around heel of right foot with right thumb on the inside, and right middle finger on the outside. Hold points three (3) seconds. Repeat on the left Achilles' tendon and heel, using your left thumb and middle finger.

POSITION 32

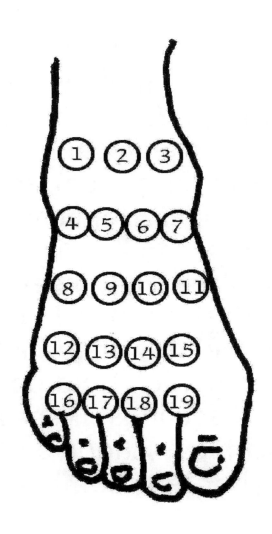

POSITION 32: Press **POINTS 1**
through **5** on right instep (top of
foot) with left thumb. Hold each
point one (1) second. Switch to left
instep and press **POINTS 1** through
5 using your right thumb.

POSITION 33

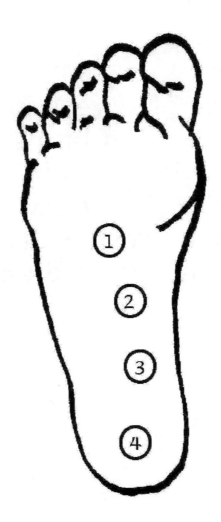

POSITION 33: Push the person's toes on right foot back lightly with the heel of left hand. Press **POINTS 1** through **4** with right thumb. Hold each point one (1) second. With the knuckles of your right hand rub down the right sole of foot to heel one (1x) time. Repeat on left foot, using left thumb and knuckles. Then facing the bottom of person's feet simultaneously lift and shake all five (5) toes one at a time between your thumbs and pointer fingers. Shake each toe one (1) second.

POSITION 34

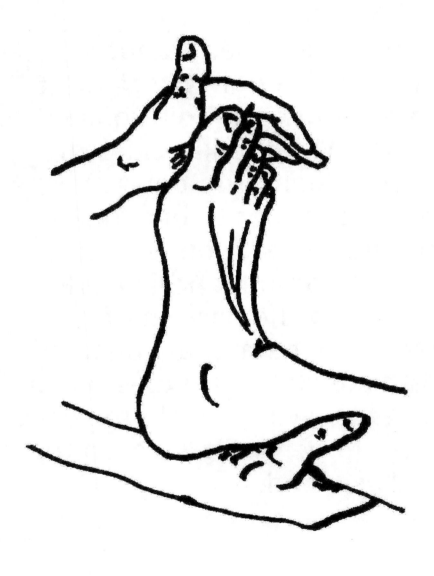

POSITION 34: Hold right ankle in palm of right hand. With heel of left hand gently push toes forward. Place palm of left hand on top of foot and gently push down. Repeat movement four (4x) times. Hold left ankle in palm of left hand. With heel of right hand gently push toes forward. Place palm of right hand on top of foot and gently push down. Repeat movement four (4x) times.

POSITION 35

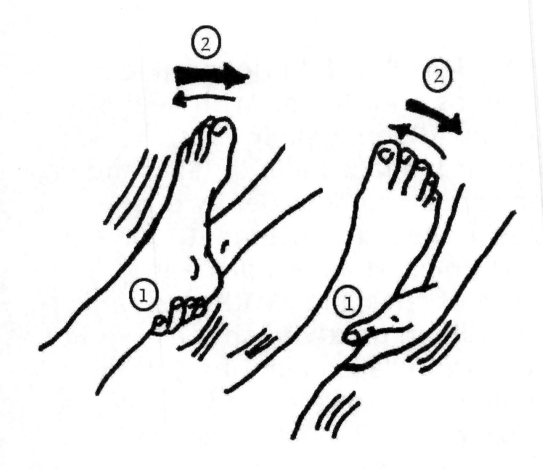

POSITION 35: Place palms of hands under both ankles at **POINTS 1**, and pull towards yourself, shaking the feet vigorously to the right and then the left, counting to seven (7). Keep the palms of your hands under the ankles, rotate both feet from the left to the right. Rotate in each direction four (4x) times. Then simultaneously raise both feet up about eight (8) inches and then back down, four (4x) times. (This move relieves stress and tension in lower back).

POSITION 36

POSITION 36: Rub hands together and place right palm on left thigh and left palm on right thigh at **POINTS 1.** Hold three (3) seconds then wipe down over the knees, shins, feet and toes at **POINTS 2** three (3x) times. (Shake your hands after each wipe).

POSITION 37

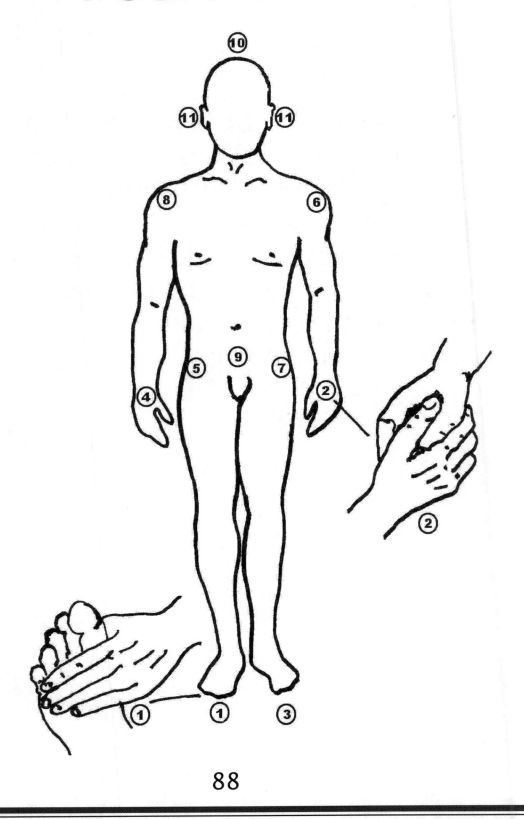

POSITION 37: Move to the left side of the person. Rub your hands together, place left palm on **POINT 1** (ball of foot) right palm on **POINT 2,** hold seven (7) seconds. (Shake your hands). Move to right side, rub hands together, place right palm on **POINT 3,** left palm on **POINT 4,** hold seven (7) seconds. (Shake your hands). Move back to left side, rub your hands together, place left palm on **POINT 5** right palm on **POINT 6,** hold seven (7) seconds. Move back to right side rub your hands together, place your right palm on **POINT 7,** left palm on **POINT 8,** hold seven (7) seconds. (Shake your hands). Remain at right side, rub hands together, place right palm on **POINT 9,** left palm on **POINT 10,** hold seven (7) seconds. (Shake your hands). Stand at crown of person's head, place your hands over the ears **POINTS 11,** hold seven (7) seconds. Press **POINT 10** at top of head with right thumb, hold 0ne (1) second. This aligns all chakras.

POSITION 38

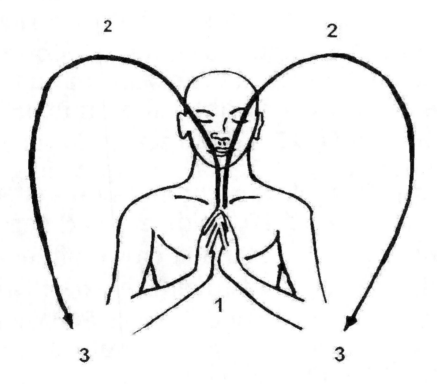

POSITION 38: Have the person lie on their right side in the fetus position facing you. Take a deep breathe and place your hands together in a prayer posture in front of your heart. Move from **POINT 1,** spreading your hands apart with palms up receiving the Prana or Life-Force, at **POINTS 2.** Lower your arms with palms still facing up to **POINTS 3** over the person for three (3) seconds. Then face your palms down over the person's body for three (3) seconds, thus filling the person with healing Life-Force.

POSITION 39

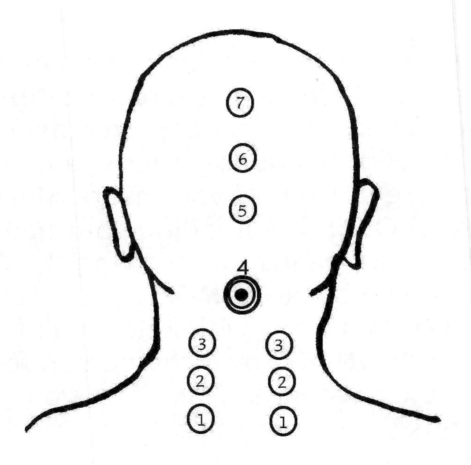

POSITION 39: With the person face down, stand at the person's left and massage **POINTS 1, 2 & 3** on both sides of back of neck with right thumb and middle finger. Massage each point three (3x) times. Press **POINT 4**, the triple burner, with right thumb three (3x) times. Press **POINTS 5, 6 & 7** on back of head with right thumb. Hold points for three (3) seconds.

POSITION 40

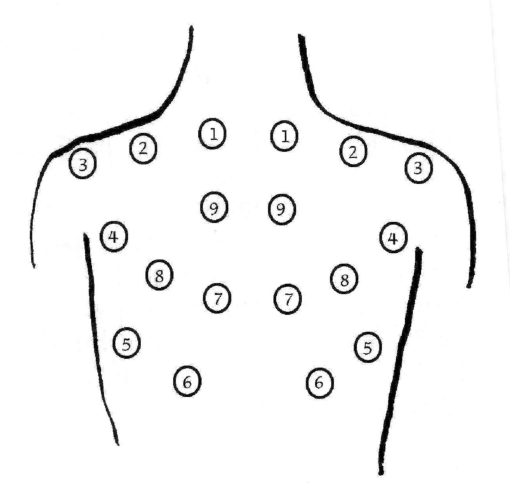

94

POSITION 40:   With both thumbs, simultaneously press **POINTS 1** through **9** on both sides of the spine. Hold each point three (3) seconds. Massage the entire back with fingertips, heels and palms of both hands.

POSITION 41

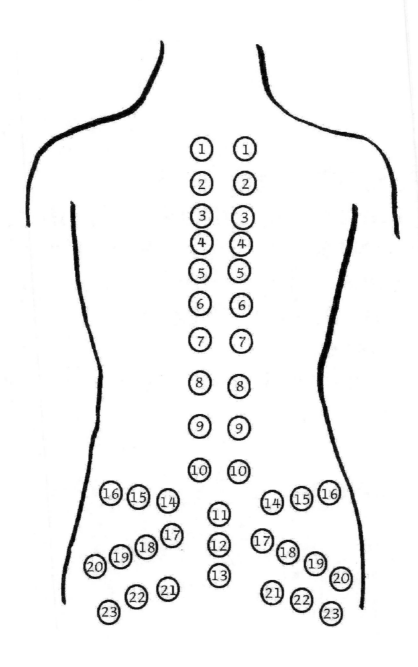

POSITION 41: With both thumbs, simultaneously press **POINTS 1** through **10** on both sides of the spine. Hold each point three (3) seconds. With both thumbs together, lightly press **POINTS 11** through **13**. Hold each point three (3) seconds. Then with thumbs apart, lightly press **POINTS 14** through **23**. Hold each point three (3) seconds.

POSITION 42

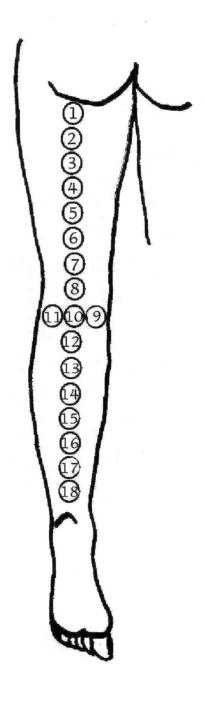

POSITION 42: Simultaneously press **POINTS 1** through **18** on the back of legs with your thumbs. Still standing at the person's left side, with the sides of your hands lightly karate chop the sole of the right foot up the leg to the middle of the back, down the right leg over the sole back up the leg to the middle of the back, down the right leg over the sole, repeat three (3) times. Continue karate chops from the waist up the spine to the base of neck, down the right side of person's back, then back up the right side. Go down the left side and back up the left side. Then go down the spine to the lower back. Continue chopping across right shoulder, down the arm over the hand back up the arm across the left shoulder down the left arm over the hand back up the arm to the base of the neck chopping up the back of neck over the top of head back to the base of neck. The chopping movement stimulates the persons nervous system.

POSITION 43

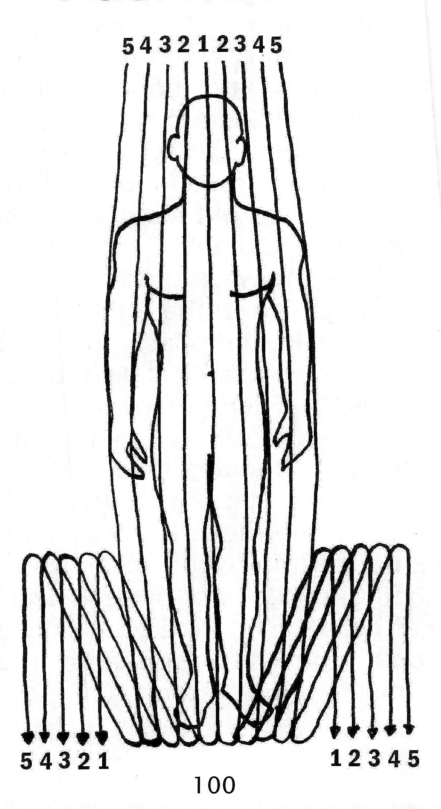

5 4 3 2 1 2 3 4 5

5 4 3 2 1   1 2 3 4 5

POSITION 43: (This is a **WIPE DOWN,** it cleanses and clears your aura). Have the person stand facing you. Place your hands together palms down about four (4) inches above the person's head at **POINT 1**. Wipe down meridian **1** to feet. (Shake your hands). Return to top of head, spread hands palms down over **POINTS 2,** wipe down the second meridian to the feet. (Shake your hands). Return to top of head, spread your hands palms down, and repeat the wipe down process over **POINTS 3, 4** and **5**. Then stand behind the person repeat the wipe down at the person's back following the same meridian points as the front. (Shake your hands). Return to front of person, place your hands together palms down over **POINT 1**. Wipe down meridian **1** to the feet five (5) times (Shake your hands).

POSITION 44

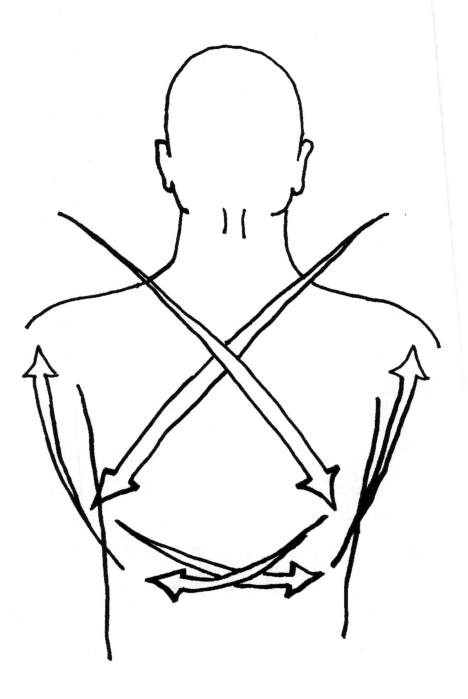

POSITION 44: Return to the back of the person, rub your hands together and place them on the end of each shoulder for seven (7) seconds. Then raise your hands about four (4) inches above the shoulders, hold three (3) seconds. Ttake one step to back, make a criss-cross motion with your arms and hands behind the back seven (7) times.

POSITION 45

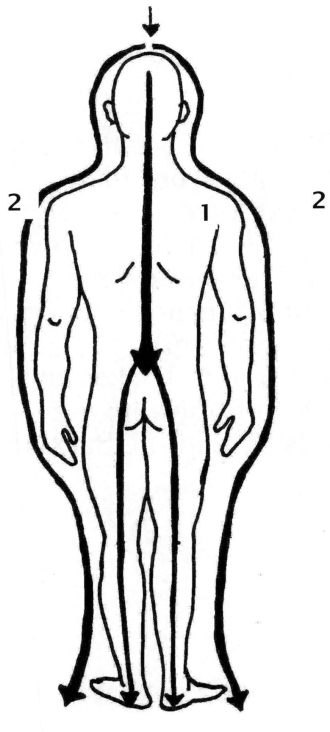

POSITION 45: Still standing behind the person, place your hands together, palms down, on top of their head. Wipe down the person's back and legs at **POINTS 1** to the floor. (Shake your hands). Again place your hands, palms down, on the top of their head. Simultaneously wipe down the sides of the head at **POINTS 2** down to the floor. (Shake your hands). Return to the front of person, rub your hands together and repeat POSITIONS **44** and **45**.

POSITION 46

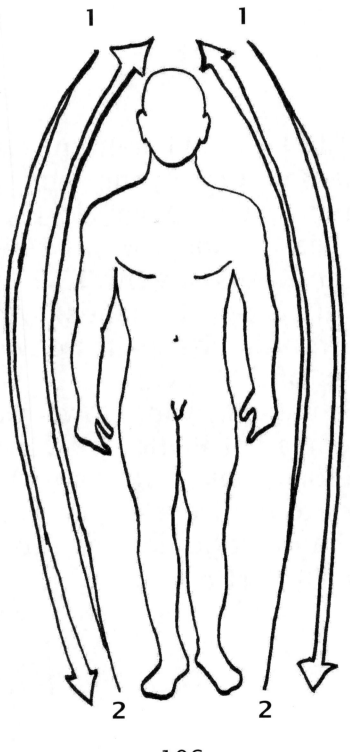

POSITION 46: (This is **CLEARING** and **SEALING THE AURA**). Remain at front of person, rub your hands together spread them apart raising them over **POINTS 1** and wipe down the outside of the person's body to the floor, return to **POINTS 2** at top of persons head. Then stand at the person's side and repeat clearing and sealing the aura front and back. Return to front of person and place your right thumb on their third eye chakra and spread your fingers on top of head. Hold three (3) seconds. "This clears and seals the person's auric field.

Experiences in Auric Polarization

My first real experience in Auric Polarization began with my first real client. I had been giving Auric Polarizations to friends and family for over a year, with favorable results. Everyone loved the polarity work and felt the difference in their stress levels. They were feeling calm, sure of themselves and more balanced. I freely shared with them the Energy that all of us have available to us if we are willing to be open channels of the Light. More and more people came, and then recommended me to others.

One morning a woman phoned me in great distress. Usually I would hand the phone to my wife, who was the one who did all the talking when it came to women and their problems. I always shied away from such confrontations, especially emotional issues. My wife, however, would not let me slip out of this one. "You are going to speak with her, John. Now is the time to begin your work." So I took a deep breath, and managed to calm the woman down. I asked her when she would like to come over for an Auric Polarization. Her answer was an immediate "Now!"

When Anna arrived at my door, she was hysterical. Her life was a mess. Her husband was filing for a divorce, she was an alcoholic, and her children were dealing with mental and emotional issues as well. She had no skills, no place to go, and no one to talk with. A friend, who had been in a similar mental and emotional state and received Auric Polarization work from me, gave my number to Anna. So there she stood, a person in need of balance, peace of mind, and calm.

I immediately gave her a trauma drain and she calmed down. We talked for a while about the issues in her life, and then I gave her an Auric Polarization.

She left smiling. The next time I saw her, a few months later, she had joined AA, was thinking about going to school, and was dealing with the children much better. In, fact she brought her son over for an Auric Polarization. He had taken some psychedelics and had what doctors called a "psychotic episode". They had him on "psyche drugs" to help him deal with his depression and suicidal tendencies, as they put it.

When David walked in the door he looked like a zombie. When I asked him to lie down on the floor, he slumped down and curled up in a ball like a baby. He was barely coherent from all the prescription drugs. I treated him, and after the Auric Polarization, he was much clearer. He came over a few more times for polarity treatments and we would talk. After that, I didn't see or hear from him for about six months. Then I received a phone call from him. He was up at college and doing great. He was back in sports again and doing well in school. He wasn't on the medication any more and wasn't feeling depressed or suicidal. In the last year I've heard from his mom, who is now a friend as well as an occasional client. She says David is still doing great. Seeing both of them joyous and smiling and moving forward with their lives, is my greatest reward.

Another experience I would like to share with you happened with my cousin. He was an advanced alcoholic and was found in a state near death. My wife and mother both suggested that I go see him because he wasn't expected to live through the night. So, I went. I saw my cousin lying there; his body all twisted up in a knot. His face contorted in excruciating pain. He was swollen all over his face and body from his failing liver. He had been put in a hospice room to die. I began the Auric Polarization, and as I beamed the Love and Light energy into him he gazed up at me with the most peculiar look on his face. He stared into my eyes as if I was some wondrous being. I watched as his body began to relax with each movement of my hands. When I reached his feet, he stared at me again in the same peculiar way. I finished up just as one of my cousin's friends walked in to the room. His friend asked him how he was doing. "Cuz did the work!" was my cousins reply. I just smiled and quietly left the room. Two days later my cousin was out of the hospital and walking around town. Unfortunately he did not heed his body's warnings and passed on a year later.

There are numerous cases that I could expound upon, but I would rather let some of my clients express how Auric Polarization has affected their lives.

®®®

"I met John when I was twenty years old. At that point in my life I was looking back on a journey of experiences where I had encountered situations like: chemical dependency among my family members, abuse, rape, and abortion. I had become a victim of my own experiences and created a self-imposed prison of fear. I developed insecurities, anxiety, a critical attitude, self-pity, anger, and overall disappointment about my life. I also developed an inner strength that wanted to persevere and learn and search out the meaning of life. I was strong-willed, and pioneering, so with the right push I could be guided toward a new perception.

The new perception began when a friend saw the trouble I was going through and decided to bring me to meet John and Charlene Van Crump. When I met them they invited me with open arms and love; they were ready to help me. John started telling me about the Auric Polarization. It was hard to believe at first; the concepts of the healing method seemed too metaphysical and spiritual for the conventional ways I had learned. I was a skeptic, so I paid attention with caution. John soon began an Auric Polarization on me and I could feel the energy right away. I couldn't believe it. My body was actually releasing energy blockages from John's touch.

I wasn't exactly sure how I felt after the Polarity, but I definitely felt different. The real surprise came the next morning. I woke up feeling like a completely different person. Overwhelmed by this new feeling, I was excited to learn more from John and receive his guidance through my perception. John extended his heart to me and continued to treat me with his methodology, and further became one of my greatest teachers.

I am now twenty-three years old and have changed my life into something special. I am a college student focusing on Communications and Psychology. I have developed my talents in music and art, and am fulfilling my divine purpose of "Light worker". I have re-defined the circumstances that I had encountered in my life and I have learned to share my understandings and can be empathetic with people. Meeting John and experiencing the Auric Polarization helped me to get my life in order and gave me a wonderful perception of growing and learning. I attribute the change in my life to my brother, John, for the Light he has brought in to my life." Thank You!

Lisa Taylor,

Riverhead,,N.Y.

"Trying to recall my first Auric Polarization or polarity is almost like trying to recall my birth…. That time in my life when I first met John and Charlene was a time of great awakening for me ~ becoming aware of the great potential inside all of us. A series of John's polarities over a season in my life released many physical, emotional, spiritual and mental blockages. By freeing up my breathing, releasing artistic abilities I didn't know I possessed, and giving me a clarity of vision. It also allowed for the opening of the realm of positive manifestation in my life ~ and set a new way of being into motion. The polarities have touched and moved me in such a way as no single methodology could. John, being a totally open conduit to the Universal Flow, could sense where to direct more energy for healing and clearing ~ even without prompting as to what specific area I needed work on. There is a specific rhythm to the order of movement which fosters a meditative state. While at the same time, each session is always a different experience. One common thread is the instant insertion into an altered state of consciousness ~ a place of healing, Love and stillness. I thank the Universal Flow for the honor of being part of this cosmic family and John for having the vision of giving the power of healing back to everyone. May we all take the healing of each other and the planet into our hands."

Heide Dohn,
Bisbee, Az.

"I experienced complete relaxation and a deep meditative state that brought my whole being into harmony. Afterwards I could breathe better and think more clearly."

Cyla Bagolan,
Southampton, N.Y.

"The Auric Polarization is an experience that brings you a total balance in all aspects – emotional, mental, spiritual and physical. This is a unique technique that clears blocked energies in areas where you're not conscious about and that never get worked out.

During one session, my whole life was revealed – flashes of when I was a little baby, a little girl, a big girl, a teenager and my early adulthood. This experience contained important information, just enough for me to figure out and release the emotions that were blocked at that certain time in my life.

It was such a real experience with the past, that then I was able to free myself from these past blockages and continue my life."

Christine Magro,
Brazil, South America

"Auric Polarization has had a positive and lasting effect in my life. After a session I feel balanced, relaxed and full of energy. Polarity also had an amazing effect on my grandmother when she was dying of cancer in 1998. Her spirits were lifted and she was able to eat and sleep after a treatment with John. She was so happy she didn't want John to leave her side.

Since I started receiving Polarity work my mind and body have been functioning on a more productive level. I hope everyone can experience an Auric Polarization at some point in his or her life time. It feels really good, and it can change your life."

Sincerely,
Laverne Schaefer,
Southampton, N.Y.

P.S.

"I would like to thank John for all the polarity work he has done on me. He spreads love and light to everyone he touches. God bless you John, you are an inspiration to us all!"

GLOSSARY

Achilles tendon - large tendon that attaches the heel bone to
        the calf muscles of the legs

Aura - a invisible energy field that surrounds the physical
        body

Chakras - are whirling energy centers that control and
        supply energy to the vital organs of the physical body

Bioplasmic – a living energy body made of invisible
        positive and negative particles of matter

Bioplasmic debris – blocked energy restricting the normal
        flow of life-force to the body's vital organs

Electro-magnetic field – a force field associated with both
        electric and magnetic compounds in motion
        around the human body

Energy – the results of the movement of electron (-) and
        protons (+) in every substance in the universe, known
        as electrical current flow between atoms

Life Force – the primal energy all form receives from d,
        our source

Meridians – Chinese energy pressure points on the
        physical body

Nadis – Hindus energy pressure points on the physical
        body

Occipital cavities – located on either side of the base of the
        skull and the top of the neck where the spinal column
        connects with the brain

Polarity – is a pattern in the universal law, that every substance
        in nature must have north and south poles

Reflexology – is a method for activating all the major glands,
        organs and body parts through the feet using finger pressure

and pressure meridians

Reiki – the use of the Universal Life force energy that naturally flows through our hands

Shiatzu – the word is from two Japanese characters, (shi) meaning finger , (atzu) meaning pressure, together they mean finger pressure

Vertebrae' – bones that make up the spinal column

BIBLIOGRAPHY

Andrews, Ted. **How to Heal with Color**. St. Paul, Minnesota: Llewellyn Publications, 1993.

Bergson, Anika and Tuchak, Uladimir. **Shiatzu: Japanese Pressure Point Massage**. New York, New York: Pinnacle Books, Inc., 1976.

Clark, Linda A. **Color Therapy**. Old Greenwich, Connecticut: The Devin Adair Company, 1982.

Gordon, Richard. **Your Healing Hands**. Oakland, California: Wingbow Press, 1994.

Judith, Anodea. **Wheels of Life**. St. Paul, Minnesota: Llewellyn Publications, 1995.

Kargere, Audrey. **Color and Personality**. York Beach, Maine: Samuel Weiser, Inc., 1990.

Krieger, Delores. PhD., R.N. **The Therapeutic Touch**. New York, New York: Prentice Hall Press, 1986.

Norman, Laura. **Feet First**. New York, New York: Fireside Book Publishing, 1988.

Rand, William Lee. **Reiki (The Healing Touch)**. Southfield, Michigan: Vision Publications, 1995.

Sui, Choa Kok. **Pranic Healing**. York Beach, Maine: Samuel Weiser, Inc., 1990

Thibodeau, Gary A., PhD. **Structure and Function of the Body, Ninth Edition**. Baltimore, Maryland: Mosby Year Book Inc. 1992.

John Van Crump is a Reiki Master Teacher and a 20 year student of Metaphysics. He lives on Long Island with his artist wife Charlene.

He currently teaches and practices **Auric Polarization** at his home on the South Shore of Long Island, New York.

You can e-mail John at: johncrump48@yahoo.com

Auric Polarization is a combination of **Polarity Therapy** (balancing the Electro-magnetic field or aura that surrounds the physical body), **Reiki** (energy work), **Shiatsu** (acupressure) and **Reflexology** (foot massage).

- Learn about **Chakras** (whirling vortices of energy known for thousands of years by East Indians as the energy centers of the body that control the different organs of the body).
- Learn how **color** affects the body, and how it can be used to restore balance to the body.
- Learn about the **4 Lower Bodies** (mental, emotional, physical and etheric) and how they affect well being.
- This book gives a step by step guide with pictures and instructions on how to give an **Auric Polarization**. So easy to read and understand that even a child can learn how to give one.
- Chock full of useful information that can be used in everyday life.
- Learn how to get rid of a headache using just you hands.
- Help relieve stress, trauma and tension with a **Trauma Drain**.
- Clear, cleanse and seal auras with an **Auric Wipe Down**.

Years of work have gone into this book, simplifying and synthesizing these 4 disciplines, so that anyone can learn how to help others with their "healing hands".